A GUIDE TO
SCOTS BIRD NAMES

Text by Robin Jackson
Illustrations by David Mitchell

DEDICATION

To Nancy, Ian and Heather

ODE TO THE GOWDSPINK

Frae fields whare Spring her sweets has blawn
Wi' caller verdure o'er the lawn,
The gowdspink comes in new attire
The brawest 'mang the whistling choir,
That, ere the sun can clear his ein,
Wi', glib notes sane the simmer's green.

Sure Nature herried mony a tree,
For spraings and bonny spats to thee;
Nae mair the rainbow can impart
Sic glowing ferlies o' her art,
Whase pencil wrought its freaks at will
On thee the sey-piece o' her skill.
Nae mair through straths in simmer dight
We seek the rose to bless our sight;
Or bid the bonny wa'-flowers sprout
On yonder ruin's lofty snout.
Thy shining garments far outstrip
The cherries upo' Hebe's lip,
And fool the tints that Nature chose
To busk and paint the crimson rose.

'Mang men, wae's-heart! we aften find
The brawest drest want peace of mind,
While he that gangs wi' ragged coat
Is weil contentit wi' his lot.
Whan wand wi' glewy birdlime's set,
To steal far aff your dautit mate,
Blyth wad ye change your cleething gay
In lieu of lav'rock's sober grey.

ODE TO THE GOWDSPINK cont.

In vain thro' woods you sair may ban
Th' envious treachery of man,
That, wi' your gowden glister ta'en,
Still hunts you on the simmer's plain,
And traps you 'mang the sudden fa's
O' winter's dreary dreepin snaws.
Now steekit frae the gowany field,
Frae ilka fav'rite houff and bield,
But mergh, alas! to disengage
Your bonny bouck frae fettering cage,
Your free-born bosom beats in vain
For darling liberty again.
In window hung, how aft we see
Thee keek around at warblers free,
That carrol saft, and sweetly sing
Wi' a' the blythness of the spring?
Like Tantalus they hing you here
To spy the glories o' the year;
And tho' you're at the burnie's brink,
They douna suffer you to drink.

Ah, Liberty! thou bonny dame,
How wildly wanton is thy stream,
Round whilk the birdies a' rejoice,
An' hail you wi' a gratefu' voice.
The gowdspink chatters joyous here,
And courts wi' gleesome sangs his peer:
The mavis frae the new-bloom'd thorn
Begins his lauds at earest morn;

ODE TO THE GOWDSPINK cont.

And herd lowns louping o'er the grass,
Need far less fleetching till their lass,
Than paughty damsels bred at courts,
Wha thraw their mou's, and take the dorts:
But, reft of thee, fient flee we care
For a' that life ahint can spare.
The gowdspink, that sae lang has kend
Thy happy sweets (his wonted friend),
Her sad confinement ill can brook
In some dark chamber's dowy nook:
Tho' Mary's hand his nebb supplies,
Unkend to hunger's painfu' cries,
Ev'n beauty canna cheer the heart
Frae life, frae liberty apart;
For now we tyne its wonted lay,
Sae lightsome sweet, sae blythly gay.

Thus Fortune aft a curse can gie,
To wyle us far frae liberty:
Then tent her syren smiles wha list,
I'll ne'er envy your girnal's grist;
For whan fair freedom smiles nae mair,
Care I for life? Shame fa' the hair:
A field o'ergrown wi' rankest stubble,
The essence of a paltry bubble.

Robert Fergusson (1750-1774)

In mery May, quhen medis springis,
And foullis in the forestis singis,
And nychtingales thare notis newis.

from The Buik of Alexander
Prologue to the Avowis of Alexander
John Barbour [c. 1320-1395]

Introduction

The publication of a list of Scots bird names should have an appeal to a wide audience: the dedicated bird watcher, the student of the Scots language, the amateur historian interested in Scottish culture, the holiday visitor to Scotland and the casual reader.

The list of Scots bird names presented in the Guide results from a fusion of two quite unconnected interests: ornithology and the Scots language. No extravagant claim is made that the list is a definitive one, indeed one of the reasons for publishing it is to encourage readers to add to it. If readers respond to this invitation in sufficient numbers, a much more comprehensive list will eventually be produced.

Most readers will be familiar with the work of the Royal Society for the Protection of Birds, one of Britain's most popular and successful charities, which is dedicated to preserving bird species and conserving habitats. Perhaps a good case could be made for the creation of a society which aims to preserve Scots bird names, for they too run the risk of disappearing and being lost for ever.

The Mavis and the Merle beginnis to mell;
The Lark on loft, with uther birdis haill,
Than drawis furth ffra derne, over down and daill.

The Preiching of the Swallow
Robert Henryson [c. 1420 - c. 1490]

Scots language

The publication of this list is timely for it coincides with a
revival in interest in the Scots language. Indeed, one of the
purposes of the list is to show the reader (Scot or non-Scot)
that Scots is a living language and one that merits our serious
attention. And bird names provide a treasure trove for anyone
interested in the Scots language. A particularly encouraging
feature of this revival is a growing recognition of the Scots
language as a legitimate area of study within the school
curriculum. For too long, the Scots language has been
regarded as an inferior cousin of standard English and has
not been recognised as a language in its own right. Rather
too much emphasis has been paid to the distinctiveness of
the Scottish legal, educational, political and cultural traditions
and too little to that single defining characteristic that sets
one nation apart from another - its language.

General observations

There are a number of brief observations that can be made
about the list. Not surprisingly, a high proportion of the names
are of birds usually found on heathland, moorland, mountain

In May begynnis the gowk to gaill;
In May drawis deir to doun and daill;
In May men mellis with famyny,
And ladeis meitis thair luvaris laill,
Quehen Phebus is in Gemnyn

Of May
Alexander Scott [c. 1515-c.1583]

upland and coastal fringe, the predominant Scottish habitats. What is surprising are the omissions. There is no reference to a number of birds commonly observed in Scotland - brambling, chiffchaff, coot, crossbill, coal tit, long-tailed tit, redwing, spotted flycatcher. The most obvious explanation is that these are omissions. Readers are therefore encouraged to remedy this deficiency.

What is also apparent is the often wide range of names for the same bird - 27 names for the chaffinch and 17 names for the yellowhammer. This reflects regional dialect variations and, possibly, fossilised spelling errors. One feature of the list which is likely to annoy the serious ornithologist is that one name can refer to quite different birds (eg, huidie craw = hooded crow, carrion crow and black headed gull; chackart = stonechat, whinchat and ring ouzel). Ornithologists are also likely to be dismayed at the tendency to group quite different birds into the same category:

Lintie	Linnet/twite
Fun lintie	Whinchat
Green lintie	Greenfinch

The thissell-cok cryis
On lovers wha lyis.
Now skaillis the skyis:
The nicht is neir gone.

The Night is Neir Gone
Captain Alexander Montgomerie [?1545-1597]

Heather lintie	Twite
Hill lintie	Twite
Rock lintie	Twite/rock pipit
Rose lintie	Linnet/lesser redpoll
Sea lintie	Rock pipit
Whin lintie	Linnet

Yalla/yallow/
  yella/yelly/
  yellow lintie
	Yellowhammer

Yella neb lintie	Twite

But perhaps this is not altogether surprising as the linnet, twite and rock pipit are notoriously difficult for the untrained observer to differentiate in the field.

A characteristic and predictable feature of Scots bird names is the large number ending in - ie.

Scots name	English name
Applie	Chaffinch
Blackie	Blackbird
Chaffie	Chaffinch
Dovekie	Black guillemot

Quhilk Sunne perceaves the little larks,
The lapwing and the snyp,
And tunes their sangs like natures clarks,
Ou'r midow, mure, and stryp.

Of the Day Estivall
Alexander Hume [?1557-1609]

Fieldie	Hedge sparrow
Goldie	Goldfinch
Hoodie craw	Hooded crow
Jackie	Jackdaw
Kittie	Kittiwake
Lavie	Razorbill
Mallie	Mallard
Norrie	Puffin
Peesie	Lapwing
Quailzie	Quail
Sandy dorbie	Sandpiper
Tystie	Black guillemot
Waggie	Pied wagtail
Yellow lintie	Yellowhammer

Origin of names

On looking through the list the reader may be prompted to wonder how some of the names have originated. In very general terms, it is possible to point to at least five explanations: (1) bird song or call; (2) appearance; (3) habitat; (4) behaviour; and (5) regional variation.

Nay mair; those greedy gleds, that iver
'Till nou had peck't Prometheus' Liver,
Forgat their prey, op't wide their throats,
And lent their lugs to Orpheus' notes.

From the Epistle to the President, Vice-Presidents, and Members of the Scottish Society of Antiquaries : On Being Chosen a Correspondent Member
Alexander Geddes [1737-1802]

1.   Bird song or call

Some of the names are clearly direct representations of the bird's call. For example, in the case of the whitethroat, we have a combination of the bird's alarm call (churr) and a description of the raised feathers on the bird's head (muffit).

Scots name	English name	Song/call
Churr muffit	Whitethroat	chairr (alarm call)
Kay/kae/kyaw	Jackdaw	kyaar/kye
Peesiewheep	Lapwing	peese-weet
Pleep	Oyster catcher	kleep, kleep (alarm call)
Spink	Chaffinch	chwink/tink
Whaup	Curlew	ooOHP

Frae fields whare Spring her sweets has blawn
Wi' verdure o'er the lawn,
The gowdspink comes in new attire,
The bravest 'mang the whistling choir

Ode to the Gowdspink
Robert Fergusson [1750-1774]

2.   *Appearance*

Perhaps one of the most unusual and unforgettable names in the list is that which describes the black and white plumage of the long tailed duck - coal and candle light. An equally evokative image is conjured up by picturing a flock of snow bunting alighting on a mountain scree, as a flurry of snowflakes.

Scots name	English name
Coal and candle light	Long tailed duck
Gooldie	Goldfinch
Red hawk	Kestrel
Snawflake	Snow bunting
Rose lintie	Linnet
Yellow lintie	Yellowhammer

8

O sweet are COILA's haughs an' woods,
When lintwhites chant amang the buds.

To William Simpson, Ochiltree
Robert Burns [1759-1796]

3.   Habitat

The habitat of the birds is frequently indicated in their name (eg, heather, moss, muir, water, whin). But then most of Scotland is made up of heather, moss, muir, water and whin!

Heather:

Heather blackie	Ring ouzel
Heather bleater	Common snipe
Heather bluitter	Common snipe
Heather cock	Black or red grouse
Heather lintie	Twite

Moss (boggy ground/moorland):

Moss bluiter	Common snipe
Moss cheeper	Meadow pipit
Moss donnack	Black headed gull
Moss duck	Mallard
Moss owl	Short eared owl
Moss sparra	Reed bunting

'Fearfu' soughs the boor-tree bank,
The rifted wood roars wild an dreary,
Loud the iron yett does clank,
The cry o howlets mak's me eerie.

O! Are ye sleepin, Maggie?
Robert Tannahill [1774-1810]

Muir (rough uncultivated heathery land):

Muir cheeper	Meadow pipit
Muir cock	Red grouse
Muir fowl	Red grouse
Muir hen	Red grouse
Muir pout	Red grouse

Water:

Water blackbird	Dipper
Water bobbie	Dipper
Water cockie	Dipper
Water craw	Dipper
Water hen	Moorhen
Water meggie	Dipper
Water pyot	Dipper
Watery wagtail	Yellow wagtail

Whin (an area of gorse):

Whin chackert	Whinchat
Whin lintie	Linnet
Whin sparrow	Hedge sparrow

Or in the gloamin' douce an' grey
The sweet-throat mavis tunes her lay

Ille Terrarum
Robert Louis Stevenson [1850-1894]

4.   *Behaviour*

The behaviour of some birds is captured by their description. *Ebb sleeper* provides a wonderfully immediate and accurate portrayal of the dunlin resting on one leg with beak tucked under wing waiting for a high tide to ebb. *Water bobbie* describes the curtseying movement of the dipper standing on a stone in the middle of a fast moving mountain stream. The presence of an eagle (*earn*) or some other avian predator may prompt the common snipe to rise and give its alarm call (bleat). Perhaps the most eloquent and poetic description of the movement of any bird is that given to the kestrel - *willie whip the wind*. We are invited to picture the kestrel facing into a strong wind and dipping and rising in a whip like motion.

Scots name	English name
Earn bleater	Common snipe
Ebb sleeper	Dunlin
Mussel picker	Oyster catcher
Water bobbie	Dipper
Willie whip the wind	Kestrel

And as for Unthank Water
That seeps through miles o' reeds and seggs,
It's aye at pilliewinkie syne
Wi' the gowdnie's eggs.

Water Music
Hugh Macdiarmid [1892-1978]

5.   *Regional variation*

Bird names can vary depending on regional location. The chaffinch provides an excellent example of this regional variation:

Angus	Shillie/shellie
Argyll	Shiltie/sheltie
Banff & Buchan	Chaffie
Caithness	Chaffinch
Dumfries & Galloway	Chilfie/brichtie
Fife	Shelliefaw
Inverness	Chaffinch
Moray & Nairn	Chaffie/chy
Perthshire	Shilfie/shelfie

There are some bird names which defy easy categorisation. The description of the robin, with its red apron, as a *mason's ghost* is particularly appealing but it belongs to no simple grouping. There are some bird names which lend themselves to a multiplicity of interpretations. Take the puffin or *sea*

The morn, the laverock shaks the air
And green comes back to the girss and gair;

The Young Man and the Young Nun
A.D. Mackie [1904-1985]

coulter or *coulterneb*. Coulter, in Scots, is the name for the blade of a plough; it is also an unflattering description for a person's nose. It is certainly the case that the puffin is not graced with the most elegant of beaks and that the beak is not dissimilar in shape to a plough blade. However anyone who has seen a puffin skimming low over the crests and troughs of the waves might be tempted to think of the bird's flight as mimicking the movement of a plough. The fact is that we don't know which is the correct explanation and therein lies the fascination. We are left to choose the explanation that appeals most to our imagination.

Conclusion

Earlier the point was made that this list resulted from the fusion of two unrelated interests: ornithology and the Scots language. As a result of this publication, it is possible that more ornithologists may become interested in the Scots language and more students of the Scots language may develop an interest in ornithology. Such a development would be mutually beneficial.

There's a reid lowe in yer cheek,
Mither, and a licht in yer ee,
And ye sing like the shuilfie in the slae,
But no' for me.

Sang
Robert Maclellan [1907-1984]

But one of the main aims of this publication is to encourage readers to contribute to a 'national collection'. The reader is invited to write down any Scots bird names that have been omitted from the list or alternative names for birds already included in the list, giving details of the geographic area in which the name is used and an indication of whether the name is still in current use.

These additions should be sent to:

Ptarmigan Press
4 Deeview Gardens
Drumoak
Aberdeenshire
AB31 5AF

Whilst the list provides an opportunity for serious study, it is also aimed at the casual reader who may be relaxing by the fire in an evening after an exhausting day's moorland, loch-side or mountain walk. The list is intended to instruct and to entertain, although Scottish Presbyterian tradition often tends to emphasise the former activity to the exclusion of the latter!

SCOTS — ENGLISH

Aigle	Eagle
Ailsa cock	Puffin
Airn	Eagle
Aiten	Partridge
Aithehen	Gray hen
Alamootie	Storm petrel
Alan	Arctic skua
Allan hawk	Great northern diver
Apple sheelie	Chaffinch
Apple shieler	Chaffinch
Applie	Chaffinch
Assilag	Storm petrel
Aulin	Arctic skua
Auten	Arctic skua
Awp	Bullfinch
Bissart	Buzzard
Bizzart	Buzzard
Blackcock	Black grouse
Black douker	Cormorant
Blackie	Blackbird
Bleater	Cock snipe/bittern
Blitter	Cock snipe/bittern
Bonxie	Great skua
Brichtie	Chaffinch
Briskie	Chaffinch
Brissel cock	Kind of game bird
Bullie	Bullfinch
Buntlin	Corn bunting
Burrough duck	Shelduck
Burrow duck	Shelduck
Bushock	Hedge sparrow
Bussard	Buzzard

Calloo	Long tailed duck
Capercailzie	Capercaille
Chackart	Stonechat/whinchat/ring ouzel
Chaffie	Chaffinch
Chafflinch	Chaffinch
Chilfie	Chaffinch
Chitty wren	Wren
Churr muffit	Whitethroat
Chy	Chaffinch
Chye	Chaffinch
Clack	Barnacle goose
Clait	Barnacle goose
Clockwret	Wheatear/stonechat
Coal and candle light	Long tailed duck
Cock o' the doos	Peregrine falcon
Col cannel week	Long tailed duck
Coot quest	Guillemot

Wren

Rook

Corbie	Raven/carrion or hooded crow/rook
Corby	Raven/carrion or hooded crow/rook
Corncraik	Corncrake/landrail
Corncrake	Corncrake/landrail
Cra	Carrion/hooded crow
Craa	Carrion/hooded crow
Craggy heron	Grey heron
Craigie heron	Grey heron
Craik	Landrail
Cran	Crane/heron/swift
Craw	Rook
Croodlin doo	Wood pigeon
Cuschett	Ringed dove/wood pigeon
Cushat	Ringed dove/wood pigeon
Cushet	Ringed dove/wood pigeon
Cushie doo	Wood pigeon
Dirten allen	Skua
Dirtin allan	Arctic skua

Dog birdie	Sooty shearwater
Doo	Dove/rock dove/feral pigeon
Dovekie	Black guillemot
Dow	Dove
Dunter duck	Eider
Earn	Eagle (white tailed or sea eagle or golden eagle)
Earn bleater	Common snipe
Ebb sleeper	Dunlin
Eirn	Eagle
Ember goose	Great northern diver
Emmer gos	Great northern diver
Ephesian	Pheasant
Erne	Eagle
Esscock	Dipper

Dipper

Faap	Curlew
Faup	Curlew
Feesian	Pheasant
Feldifare	Fieldfare/missel thrush
Feltieflier	Fieldfare/missel thrush
Feltifare	Fieldfare/missel thrush
Feltifer	Fieldfare/missel thrush
Fiddler	Sandpiper
Fieldy	Hedge sparrow
Foula hen	Great skua
Fulmar	Petrel
Fun chackert	Whinchat
Fun lintie	Whinchat
Gair fowl	Great auk
Gant	Gannet
Glaid	Kite/buzzard
Glassie gull	Glaucous gull
Gled	Kite/buzzard
Gock	Cuckoo
Golden crestie	Goldcrest
Goldie	Goldfinch
Goldspink	Goldfinch
Golk	Cuckoo
Gooldie	Goldfinch
Gorcock	Red grouse (m)
Goudspink	Goldfinch
Gowdie duck	Goldeneye
Gowdnie	Goldeneye
Gowdspink	Goldfinch
Gowk	Cuckoo
Gowkgoke	Cuckoo
Grayback	Hooded crow/herring gull (i)/lesser black backed gull
Gray cheeper	Meadow pipit
Gray hen	Black grouse (f)

Gray plover	Golden plover (summer plumage)
Gray willie	Herring gull
Greenie	Greenfinch
Green lintie	Greenfinch
Greyback	Hooded crow/herring gull (i)/lesser black backed gull
Groose	Grouse
Grund blackie	Blackbird
Gustard	Bustard
Hack	Sparrowhawk/kestrel
Harle	Goosander
Heather blackie	Ring ouzel
Heather bleater	Common snipe
Heather bluitter	Common snipe
Heather cock	Black or red grouse
Heather lintie	Twite or mountain linnet
Hedder blackie	Ring ouzel
Hedge spurdie	Hedge sparrow
Hedge spurgie	Hedge sparrow
Hegri	Grey heron
Herald deuk	Red breasted merganser
Herald duck	Goosander
Herle	Grey heron
Hern	Grey heron
Heronis saw	Grey heron
Heronshew	Grey heron
Hether blackie	Ring ouzel
Hielan paddy	Fieldfare
Highland pyot	Missel thrush
Hill lintie	Twite
Hoodie craw	Hooded crow
Hoolet	Tawny owl
Hoolit	Tawny owl
Hornie hoolet	Long eared owl
Hornie oolet	Long eared owl

Grey Heron

Horsecock	Dunlin
Horsegock	Snipe
Houlet	Tawny owl
Howlet	Tawny owl
Huidie craw	Hooded crow/carrion crow/black headed gull
Huron	Grey heron
Immer	Great northern diver
Ja	Jay
Jackie	Jackdaw
Ja-pyot	Jay
Jenny	Black guillemot (first or winter plumage)
Jenny	Heron
Jinny gray	Black guillemot (first or winter plumage)
Jinny heron	Grey heron

Joctibeet	Wheatear
Johnny norrie	Puffin
Kae	Jackdaw
Katiewren	Wren
Kay	Jackdaw
Keelie hawk	Kestrel
Killie leepie	Common sandpiper
Killie neddie	Common sandpiper
Killie needy	Common sandpiper
Kittie	Kittiewake
Kittie needy	Common sandpiper
Kittie wren	Wren
Kweet	Guillemot
Kyaw	Jackdaw
Lairag	Skylark

Kestrel

Lairick	Skylark
Lang Sandy	Grey heron
Larick	Skylark
Latower	Swallow
Laverock	Skylark
Laverok	Skylark
Laveroo	Skylark
Lavie	Guillemot/razorbill
Leam	Great northern diver
Leerie	Manx shearwater
Lintick	Linnet/twite
Lintie	Linnet/twite
Lintwhite	Linnet
Liverock	Skylark
Livrock	Skylark
Loch maa	Common gull
Loch maw	Common gull
Longie	Common guillemot
Loom	Red throated diver /guillemot
Loren	Cormorant
Maa	Common gull
Maggie	Magpie
Mairtin	House martin
Mallduck	Fulmar
Mallie	Fulmar/mallard
Mallimoke	Fulmar
Mane	Goldcrest
Marlzeon	Merlin
Marrot	Common guillemot/razorbill
Mason's ghost	Robin
Maveis	Song thrush
Mavis	Song thrush
Maw	Common gull
Meen	Goldcrest
Merl	Blackbird

Blackbird

Merle	Blackbird
Merlzeoun	Merlin
Meybird	Whimbrel
Mi	Goldcrest
Miredrum	Bittern
Mire duck	Mallard
Mire snipe	Common snipe
Mittane	Hen harrier (m)
Mitten	Hen harrier (m)
Mochrum elder	Cormorant
Mone	Goldcrest
Moon	Goldcrest
Mortoun	Guillemot or razorbill
Moss bluiter	Common snipe
Moss cheeper	Meadow pipit
Moss donnack	Black headed gull
Moss duck	Mallard
Moss owl	Short eared owl
Moss sparra	Reed bunting

Muir cheeper	Meadow pipit
Muir cock	Red grouse (m)
Muir fowl	Red grouse
Muir hen	Red grouse (f)
Muir pout	Red grouse (i)
Mussel picker	Oyster catcher
Mussill picker	Oyster catcher
Nettlecreeper	Whitethroat
Nettliecreeper	Whitethroat
Nichtingale	Nightingale
Nychtingale	Nightingale
Norie	Puffin
Norrie	Puffin
Oolit	Tawny owl
Osill	Ouzel, blackbird
Oxee	Great tit, blue tit
Pairtrik	Partridge
Paitrick	Grey partridge
Partrich	Grey partridge
Partrik	Partridge
Patie	Puffin
Patrick	Partridge
Peesie	Lapwing
Peesiewheep	Lapwing
Peesweep	Lapwing
Peewee	Lapwing
Peeweet	Lapwing
Peirtrick	Partridge
Pellile	Redshank
Perdrix	Partridge
Perma	Black headed gull
Pertridge	Partridge
Pertrik	Partridge

Pewl	Herring gull
Peyet	Magpie
Pheesant	Pheasant
Piccatarrie	Common or arctic tern, black headed gull
Pickerel	Dunlin
Picket a	Common or arctic tern, black headed gull
Pickmaw	Black headed gull
Picktarntie	Common or arctic tern, black headed gull
Pictarnie	Common or arctic tern, black headed gull
Piet	Magpie
Pikkerel	Dunlin
Pikmaw	Black headed gull
Pirr	Common tern

Black Headed Gull

Pirr maw	Black headed gull
Pleengie	Herring full (i)
Pleep	Oyster catcher, redshank
Plever	Plover
Pliver	Plover
Plover's page	Dunlin
Pluvar	Plover
Potterton hen	Black headed gull
Pule	Herring gull
Pyat	Magpie
Pyot	Magpie
Pyowl	Herring gull
Quailze	Quail/corncrake
Quaip	Curlew
Quhap	Curlew
Quink goose	Brent/greylag goose
Quit	Guillemot
Rain gos	Red throated diver
Redhawk	Merlin/kestrel
Red legged crow	Chough
Red neb	Oyster catcher
Rednebbit pussy	Puffin
Red Rab	Robin
Revin	Raven
Rockall jack	Manx shearwater
Rock lintie	Twite/rock pipit
Rood goose	Brent goose
Rose lintie	Linnet (m)/lesser redpoll
Rosignell	Nightingale
Ruik	Rook
Ruke	Rook
Rutt	Brent goose
Saandiloo	Ringed plover

Goosander

Sandy dorbie	Sandpiper
Sandy lairick	Ringed plover
Sandy laverock	Ringed plover
Sandy swallow	Sand martin
Sawneb	Goosander/red breasted merganser
Scaledrake	Sheldrake
Scarf	Cormorant/shag
Scart	Cormorant/shag
Scarth	Cormorant/shag
Scobbie	Chaffinch
Scoot	Razorbill/guillemot
Scooty alan	Arctic skua
Scop	Chaffinch
Scoppie	Chaffinch
Scotch nightingale	Woodlark/sedge warbler
Scout	Razorbill/guillemot
Scurrie	Herring gull
Sea coulter	Puffin
Sea craa	Razorbill

Sea doo	Black guillemot
Sea hen	Common guillemot
Sea lintie	Rock pipit
Sea pyot	Oyster catcher
Seed bird	Wagtail
Seed lady	Pied wagtail
Shalder	Oyster catcher
Shavie	Chaffinch
Sheelie	Chaffinch
Shelfie	Chaffinch
Shellie	Chaffinch
Shelliefaw	Chaffinch
Shilfa	Chaffinch
Shilfie	Chaffinch
Shillie	Chaffinch
Shilly	Chaffinch
Shiltie	Chaffinch

Chaffinch

Shot whaip	Curlew
Shoulfall	Chaffinch
Shuilfie	Chaffinch
Shulfie	Chaffinch
Skarf	Cormorant
Skarth	Cormorant
Skeet	Yellowhammer
Skelldrake	Sheldrake
Skirlie	Oyster catcher
Skirly wheeter	Oyster catcher
Skite	Yellowhammer
Skitterie mavie	Blackbird
Skittery feltie	Fieldfare
Skrath	Shag
Snaaie fool	Snow bunting
Snawflake	Snow bunting
Snippik	Snipe
Snowflake	Snow bunting
Snyauveflake	Snow bunting
Snyp	Common snipe
Solan goose	Gannet
Sparra	Sparrow
Sparry	Sparrow
Specht	Green woodpecker
Speug	House sparrow
Spink	Chaffinch
Spinkie	Chaffinch
Sporrow	Sparrow
Sproug	House sparrow
Sprug	House sparrow
Spug	House sparrow
Spurdie	Hedge sparrow
Spurg	House sparrow
Spurgie	House sparrow
Stanchel	Kestrel
Stanechack	Stonechat/wheatear

Curlew

Stanechacker	Stonechat/wheatear
Stanechart	Stonechat/wheatear
Stankiehen	Moorhen
Steenchack	Stonechat/wheatear
Steenchacker	Stonechat/wheatear
Stenchil	Kestrel
Stenshakker	Wheatear
Stenkle	Wheatear
Stenshik	Wheatear
Stinkle	Wheatear
Stirlin	Starling
Stirling	Starling
Stock	Sheldrake
Stock dyook	Mallard
Stock whaap	Curlew
Stonechack	Stonechat/wheatear
Stonechacker	Stonechat/wheatear
Stonechart	Stonechat/wheatear
Stonechipper	Wheatear

Stormcock	Missel thrush
Stoukannet	Sheldrake
Stuckie	Starling
Stushie	Starling
Swaabie	Great black backed gull
Swalla	Swallow
Swankie's doo	Seagull
Tammie checkie	Puffin
Tammie cheekie	Puffin
Tammie norrie	Puffin
Tammy norrie	Puffin
Tang sporrow	Rock pipit
Tang whaup	Whimbrel
Tarmachan	Ptarmigan
Tarmagan	Ptarmigan
Tarrock	Common tern/kittiwake
Teetik	Meadow pipit
Teewheet	Lapwing
Teewhip	Lapwing
Teistie	Black guillemot
Termigant	Ptarmigan
Teuchat	Lapwing
Teuchit	Lapwing
Thissell cok	Song thrush
Thristle	Song thrush
Thristle cok	Song/missel thrush
Throstle	Song/missel thrush (m)
Tibbie thiefie	Sandpiper
Tirrick	Common/arctic tern/kittiwake
Titlin	Meadow pipit
Titling	Meadow pipit
Toist	Black guillemot
Tormican	Ptarmigan
Treespeeler	Tree creeper
Tuchit	Lapwing

Turtour	Turtle dove
Tystie	Black guillemot
Waggatie wa	Pied wagtail
Waggie	Pied wagtail
Waggitie	Pied wagtail
Wallop	Lapwing
Ware goose	Brent goose
Water blackbird	Dipper
Water bobbie	Dipper
Water cock	Dipper
Water cockie	Dipper
Water craw	Dipper
Water hen	Moorhen
Water meggie	Dipper
Water pyot	Dipper
Watery wagtail	Yellow wagtail
Weeg	Kittiwake
Weet my fit	Landrail/corncrake
Whap	Curlew
Whaap	Curlew
Whaup	Curlew
Wheelie oe	Willow warbler
Wheetie	Whitethroat
Whitebeard	Whitethroat/willow warbler
Whin chacker	Whinchat
Whin chackert	Whinchat
Whin lintie	Linnet
Whin sparrow	Hedge sparrow
Whishie	Whitethroat
White hoolet	Barn owl
Whitterick	Curlew
Whusky whey beard	Whitethroat
Widd lark	Tree pipit
Willie goo	Herring gull
Willie muff	Willow warbler

Willie muffitie	Willow warbler
Willie muftie	Willow warbler
Willie wagtail	Pied wagtail
Willie whip the wind	Kestrel
Wode lark	Tree pipit
Wood lark	Tree pipit
Wunda swalla	House martin
Wuid lark	Tree pipit
Woodpecker	Treecreeper
Wud lark	Tree pipit
Wudd lark	Tree pipit
Wye	Iceland/glaucous gull
Yaldrin	Yellowhammer
Yalla lintie	Yellowhammer
Yalla yite	Yellowhammer
Yalla yorlin	Yellowhammer

Willow Warbler

Yellowhammer

Yallock	Yellowhammer
Yallow lintie	Yellowhammer
Yarlin	Yellowhammer
Yeldrin	Yellowhammer
Yella lintie	Yellowhammer
Yella neb lintie	Twite
Yella plover	Golden plover
Yelly lintie	Yellowhammer
Yella wagtail	Grey wagtail
Yellow lintie	Yellowhammer
Yern bliter	Common snipe
Yern blitter	Common snipe
Yirlin	Yellowhammer
Yirn	Eagle
Yite	Yellow hammer
Yoldrin	Yellowhammer
Yorlin	Yellowhammer

ENGLISH — SCOTS

Arctic skua

Alan
Aulin
Auten
Dirtin allan
Scooty alan

Arctic tern

Piccatarrie
Picket a
Picktarntie
Pictarnie
Tirrick

Barnacle goose

Clack
Clait

Barnacle Goose

Barn owl	White hoolet
Bittern	Bleater
	Blitter
	Miredrum
Blackbird	Blackie
	Grund blackie
	Merl
	Merle
	Osill
	Skitterie mavie
Black grouse	Blackcock
Black grouse (f)	Gray hen
	Heather cock
Black guillemot	Dovekie
	Jenny
	Jinny gray
	Sea doo
	Teistie
	Toist
	Tystie
Black headed gull	Moss donnack
	Perma
	Piccatarrie
	Picket a
	Pickmaw
	Picktarntie
	Pictarnie
	Pikmaw
	Pirr maw
	Potterton hen
	Huidie craw

Blue tit	Oxee
Brent goose	Rood goose
	Quink goose
	Rutt
	Ware goose
Bullfinch	Awp
	Bullie
Bustard	Gustard
Buzzard	Bissart
	Bizzart
	Bussard
	Glaid
	Gled
Capercaille	Capercailzie
Carrion crow	Corbie
	Corby
	Cra
	Craa
	Huidie craw
Chaffinch	Apple sheelie
	Apple shieler
	Applie
	Brichtie
	Briskie
	Chaffie
	Chilfie
	Chy
	Chye
	Scobbie
	Scop

Chaffinch	Scoppie
	Shavie
	Sheelie
	Shelfie
	Shellie
	Shelliefaw
	Sheltie
	Shilfa
	Shilfie
	Shillie
	Shilly
	Shiltie
	Shoulfall
	Shuilfie
	Shulfie
	Spink
	Spinkie
Chough	Red legged crow
Common guillemot	Longie
	Marrot
	Sea hen
Common gull	Loch maa
	Loch maw
	Maa
	Maw
Common sandpiper	Killie leepie
	Killie neddie
	Killie needy
	Kittie needy
Common snipe	Earn bleater
	Heather bleater

Cormorant

Common snipe	Heather bluitter
	Mire snipe
	Moss bluiter
	Yern bliter
	Yern blitter
Common tern	Piccatarrie
	Picket a
	Picktarntie
	Pictarnie
	Pirr
	Tarrock
	Tirrick
Cormorant	Black douker
	Loren
	Mochrum elder

Cormorant	Scarf
	Scart
	Scarth
	Skarf
	Skarth
Corn bunting	Buntlin
Corncrake	Corncraik
	Corncrake
	Quailye
	Quailze
	Weet my fit
Crane	Cran
Cuckoo	Gock
	Golk
	Gowk
	Gowkgoke
Curlew	Faap
	Faup
	Quhap
	Quhaip
	Shot whaip
	Stock whaap
	Whap
	Whaap
	Whaup
	Whitterick
Dipper	Esscock
	Water blackbird
	Water bobbie
	Water cock

Dipper	Water cockie
	Water craw
	Water meggie
	Water pyot
Dove	Doo
	Dow
Dunlin	Ebb sleeper
	Horsecock
	Pickerel
	Pikkerel
	Plover's page
Eagle	Aigle
	Airn
Eagle . golden	Earn
. sea	
. white tailed	
	Eirn
	Erne
	Yirn
Eider	Dunter duck
Feral pigeon	Doo
Fieldfare	Feldifare
	Feltieflier
	Feltifare
	Feltifer
	Hielan paddy
	Skittery feltie
Fulmar	Mallduck

Fulmar	Mallimoke
	Mallie
Game bird	Brissel cock
Gannet	Gant
	Solan goose
Glaucous gull	Glassie gull
	Wye
Goldcrest	Golden crestie
	Mane
	Meen
	Mi
	Mone
	Moon

Eider Duck

Gannet

Goldeneye	Gowdie duck
	Gowdnie
Golden plover	Gray plover
(summer plumage)	Yella plover
Goldfinch	Goldie
	Goldspink
	Gooldie
	Goudspink
	Gowdspink
Goosander	Harle
	Herald duck
	Sawneb
Gray hen	Aithehen
Great auk	Gair fowl

Great black backed gull	Swaabie
Great northern diver	Allan hawk Ember goose Emmer gos Immer Leam
Great skua	Bonxie Foula hen
Great tit	Oxee
Greenfinch	Greenie Green lintie
Green woodpecker	Specht

Goldfinch

Grouse

Grey heron	Craggy heron
	Craigie heron
	Cran
	Hegri
	Herle
	Hern
	Heronis saw
	Heronshew
	Huron
	Jenny
	Jinny heron
	Lang Sandy
Greylag goose	Quink goose
Grey wagtail	Yella wagtail
Grouse	Groose

Guillemot	Coot quest
	Kweet
	Lavie
	Loom
	Mortoun
	Quit
	Scoot
	Scout
Hedge sparrow	Bushock
	Fieldy
	Hedge spurdie
	Hedge spurgie
	Spurdie
	Whin sparrow
Hen harrier (m)	Mittane
	Mitten
Herring gull	Gray willie
	Grayback
	Greyback
	Pewl
	Pleengie
	Pule
	Pyowl
	Scurrie
	Willie goo
Hooded crow	Corbie
	Corby
	Cra
	Craa
	Grayback
	Greyback
	Hoodie craw
	Huidie craw

House martin	Mairtin
	Wunda swalla
House sparrow	Speug
	Sproug
	Sprug
	Spug
	Spurg
	Spurgie
Iceland gull	Wye
Jackdaw	Jackie
	Kae
	Kay
	Kyaw
Jay	Ja
	Ja pyot
Kestrel	Keelie hawk
	Redhawk
	Stanchel
	Stenchil
	Willie whip the wind
Kite	Glaid
	Gled
Kittiwake	Kittie
	Tarrock
	Tirrick
	Weeg
Landrail	Corncraik
	Corncrake

Landrail	Craik
	Weet my fit
Lapwing	Peesie
	Peesiewheep
	Peesweep
	Peewee
	Peeweet
	Teewheet
	Teewhip
	Teuchat
	Teuchit
	Tuchit
	Wallop
Lesser black backed gull	Grayback
	Greyback
Lesser redpoll	Rose lintie
Long eared owl	Hornie hoolet
	Hornie oolet
Long tailed duck	Calloo
	Coal and candle light
	Col cannel week
Linnet	Lintick
	Lintie
	Lintwhite
	Rose lintie
	Whin lintie
Magpie	Maggie
	Peyet
	Piet
	Pyat
	Pyot

Mallard	Mallie
	Mire duck
	Moss duck
	Stock dyook
Manx shearwater	Leerie
	Rockall jack
Meadow pipit	Gray cheeper
	Moss cheeper
	Muir cheeper
	Teetik
	Titlin
	Titling
Merlin	Marlzeon
	Merlzeoun
	Redhawk

Linnet

Meadow Pipit

Missel thrush	Feldifare
	Feltieflier
	Feltifare
	Feltifer
	Highland pyot
	Stormcock
	Thristle cok
	Throstle
Moorhen	Stankiehen
	Water hen
Mountain linnet	Heather lintie
Nightingale	Nichtingale
	Nychtingale
	Rosignell

Ouzel	Osill
Oyster catcher	Mussel picker
	Mussill picker
	Pleep
	Red neb
	Sea pyot
	Shalder
	Skirlie
	Skirly wheeter
Partridge	Aiten
	Pairtrik
	Paitrick
	Partrich
	Partrik
	Patrick
	Peirtrick
	Perdrix
	Pertridge
	Pertrik
Peregrine falcon	Cock o' the doos
Petrel	Fulmar
Pheasant	Ephesian
	Feesian
	Pheesant
Pied wagtail	Seed lady
	Waggatie wa
	Waggie
	Waggitie
	Willie wagtail

54

Plover	Plever
	Pliver
	Pluvar
Ptarmigan	Tarmachan
	Tarmagan
	Termigant
	Tormican
Puffin	Ailsa cock
	Johnny norrie
	Norie
	Norrie
	Patie
	Rednebbit pussy
	Sea coulter
	Tammie checkie
	Tammie cheekie
	Tammie norrie
	Tammy norrie
Quail	Quailze
Razorbill	Lavie
	Mortoun
	Scoot
	Scout
	Sea craa
Raven	Corbie
	Corby
	Revin
Red breasted merganser	Herald deuk
	Sawneb

Red grouse (m)	Gorcock
	Muir cock
	Muir fowl
Red grouse (f)	Muir hen
Red grouse (i)	Muir pout
Redshank	Pellile
	Pleep
Red throated diver	Loom
	Rain gos
Reed bunting	Moss sparra
Ringed dove	Cushat
	Cushet
Ring ouzel	Chackart
	Heather blackie
	Hedder blackie
	Hether blackie
Ringed plover	Saandiloo
	Sandy lairick
	Sandy laverock
Robin	Mason's ghost
	Red Rab
Rock dove	Doo
Rock pipit	Rock lintie
	Sea lintie
	Tang sporrow

Rook	Corbie
	Corby
	Craw
	Ruik
	Ruke
Sand martin	Sandy swallow
Sandpiper	Fiddler
	Sandy dorbie
	Tibbie thiefie
Seagull	Swankie's doo
Sedge warbler	Scotch nightingale

Ringed Plover

Shag	Scarf
	Scart
	Scarth
	Skrath
Sheldrake	Scaledrake
	Skelldrake
	Stock
	Stoukannet
Shelduck	Burrough duck
	Burrow duck
Short eared owl	Moss owl
Skua	Dirten allen
Skylark	Lairag
	Lairick
	Larick
	Laverock
	Laverok
	Laveroo
	Liverock
	Livrock
Snipe	Bleater
	Blitter
	Horsegock
	Snippik
	Snyp
Snow bunting	Snaaie fool
	Snawflake
	Snowflake
	Snyauveflake

Snipe

Song thrush	Maveis
	Mavis
	Thissell cok
	Thristle
	Thristle cok
	Throstle
Sooty shearwater	Dog birdie
Sparrow	Sparra
	Sparry
	Sporrow
Sparrowhawk	Hack
Starling	Stirlin
	Stirling
	Stuckie
	Stushie

Stonechat	Chackart
	Clockwret
	Stanechack
	Stanechacker
	Stanechart
	Steenchack
	Steenchacker
	Stonechack
	Stonechacker
	Stonechart
Storm petrel	Alamootie
	Assilag
Swallow	Latower
	Swalla
Swift	Cran

Swallow

Tawny owl	Hoolet
	Hoolit
	Howlat
	Howlet
	Oolit
Tree creeper	Treespeeler
	Woodpecker
Tree pipit	Widd lark
	Wode lark
	Wood lark
	Wuid lark
	Wud lark
	Wudd lark
Turtle dove	Turtour
Twite	Heather lintie
	Hill lintie
	Lintick
	Lintie
	Rock lintie
	Yella neb lintie
Wagtail	Seed bird
Wheatear	Clockwret
	Joctibeet
	Stanechack
	Stanechacker
	Stanechart
	Steenchack
	Steenchacker
	Stenkle
	Stenshakker

Wheatear

Wheatear	Stenshik
	Stinkle
	Stonechack
	Stonechacker
	Stonechart
	Stonechipper
Whimbrel	Meybird
	Tang whaup
Whinchat	Chackart
	Fun chackert
	Fun lintie
	Whin chacker
	Whin chackert
Whitethroat	Churr muffit
	Nettlecreeper

	Nettliecreeper
	Wheetie
	Whishie
	Whitebeard
	Whusky whey beard
Willow warbler	Wheelie oe
	Whitebeard
	Willie muff
	Willie muffitie
	Willie muftie
Woodlark	Scotch nightingale
Wood pigeon	Croodlin doo
	Cushat
	Cushet
	Cushie doo
Wren	Chitty wren
	Katie wren
	Kittie wren
Yellowhammer	Skeet
	Skite
	Yaldrin
	Yalla lintie
	Yalla yite
	Yalla yorlin
	Yallock
	Yallow lintie
	Yarlin
	Yeldrin
	Yella lintie
	Yellow lintie
	Yelly lintie
	Yirlin

Yite
Yoldrin
Yorlin

Yellow wagtail   Watery wagtail